result, some of the Canadian rules were applied to the American game, and today only eleven players per team are allowed on the field at one time.

Although the game was now widespread across the United States, everyone played to their own rules, and something

Walter Camp, football coach at Yale University, who helped to draw up the new playing rules

had to be done. At a convention in 1876, national playing rules were at last drawn up and the game began to take its presentday form.

As early as 1892, players were being paid to play the game. It wasn't until 1920 that an organised professional l

Americ
Associa
name v
Footbal
is still known today.

The NFL symbol shown is now known worldwide

American football is a team game that is violent in its physical clashes and packed with explosive incidents, but it is also played under strict rules. It is a battle of territories and possession which is exciting to watch.

Over four million people in Britain watch the game on television every week during the season – and ten thousand people have started to play it.

This book is a basic guide to American football, one of the world's most spectacular sports.

Measurements in this book follow American usage.
The equivalent metric measurements are (approximately) –

1 yard	= 0.914 metre	
1 foot	= 0.305 metre	
1 inch	= 2.5 centimetres	
1 pound	= 0.454 kilogram	
1 ounce	= 28 grams	
1 stone	= 14 pounds	= 6.35 kilograms

British Library Cataloguing in Publication Data

Brett, Mick
   American football.
   1. American football – For children
I. Title   II. Malone, Jerry
796.332

   ISBN 0-7214-1013-8

First edition

Published by Ladybird Books Ltd Loughborough Leicestershire UK
Ladybird Books Inc Auburn Maine 04210 USA

TM & © 1988 NFL Properties (UK) Ltd
© LADYBIRD BOOKS LTD MCMLXXXVIII

Printed in England

AMERICAN FOOTBALL

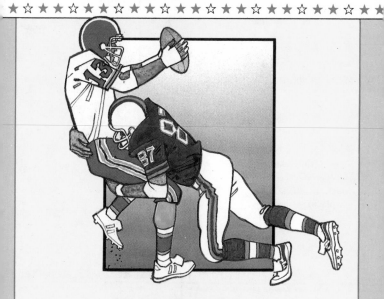

by Mick Brett

illustrated by Jerry Malone

Ladybird Books

FIELD OF PLAY

The field of play is sometimes called the 'gridiron' because it looks like a grid. The playing surface is either grass or artificial turf. Terms used to describe the field of play are:

End Line

The goal posts are above the centre of each end line.

Border

A 6 feet wide border goes round the field.

End Zone

The 10 yard scoring area.

Hash Marks

These form a channel down the centre of the field within which the officials spot (or place) the ball.

Goal Line

A stripe 8 inches wide.

Restraining Line

Everyone not taking part in the game must remain outside this line.

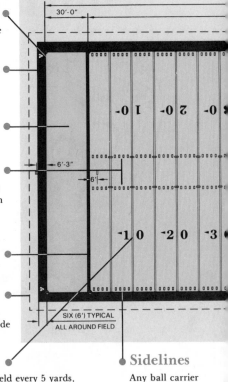

Yard Lines

There are lines across the field every 5 yards, and field numbers appear every 10 yards. An arrow next to each field number points in the direction of the nearest goal line, except at the 50 yard line which is halfway.

Sidelines

Any ball carrier who steps beyond the sideline is said to be out of bounds.

4

Goal Posts

An 18.5 ft wide crossbar is suspended 10 ft above the end line, between two uprights.

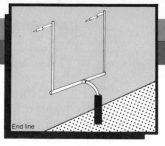

End line

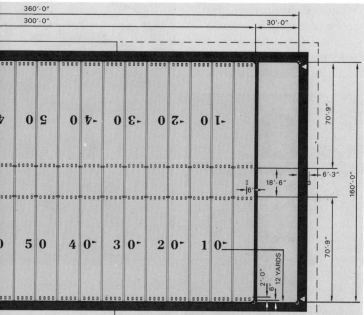

360'-0"
300'-0"
30'-0"

70'-9"

6'-3"

160'-0"

18'-6"

6'

70'-9"

2'-0"
6"
12 YARDS

7 0 5 0 4 0 3 0 2 0 1

0 5 0 4 0 3 0 2 0 1 0

Team Benches

These must be at least 10 yards from the field of play.

The Ball

The ball is a rubber bladder enclosed in a pebble-grained leather. It weighs 14 to 15 ounces.

Wilson
Official NFL

5

EQUIPMENT

Here is a player fully equipped for action. He is wearing up to eighteen pieces of padded equipment, and the complete protective uniform weighs about 15 lbs. Kitting out a player is very expensive –

but also very necessary to protect him from serious injury.

But before he puts on his protective uniform, a player has to be 'taped up' by his trainer. He may have his hands, wrists, arms, elbows, shoulders, knees, ankles and feet all taped up – or only some of these, depending on what he is expected to do during the game. Each team uses over a hundred *miles* of tape in the course of a season!

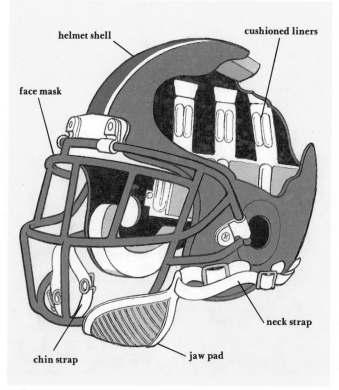

helmet shell

cushioned liners

face mask

neck strap

chin strap

jaw pad

The most important piece of a player's armour is his helmet, because the head receives a great deal of contact during a game. The helmet weighs about 3 lbs

OBJECTIVE

In American football, the winning team is the one with the most points at the end of the set playing time, which is sixty minutes. To gain points, one team must take the ball into the opponents' end zone for a touchdown or kick a field goal.

Although each team has 45 players, only 11 are allowed on the field at a time. The *offensive* squad takes the ball up the field. When the ball is lost, the *defensive* squad takes over. A third *specialist* squad is brought into play for kicking situations.

British born Mick Luckhurst kicks off for the Atlanta Falcons

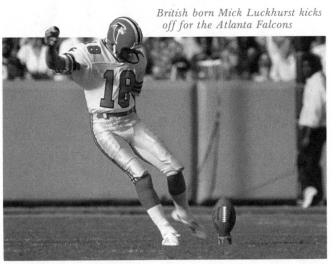

The ball is placed upright on a plastic tee on the kicking team's 35 yard line. The kick must travel at least 10 yards forward unless touched by an opponent, and the rest of the team must be behind the kicker when the ball is struck

The game starts with a *kickoff*. Which team takes the first kickoff is decided before the game by the captains tossing a coin. The winner decides whether his team will kickoff or receive the kickoff, and also which goal his team will defend. The loser has the same choice in the second half.

The kickoff starts the play at the beginning of each half, and after every score. The team kicking-off try to put the ball into enemy territory, while the receiving team try to take it back upfield.

From the kickoff, the ball is said to be 'dead' if it goes beyond the end zone, or if the receiver catches it in the end zone and touches the ground with his knee. A 'touchback' is called, and the ball is put into play from the receiving team's 20 yard line. If the receiver advances upfield with the ball, however, his teammates will try to block attempts to tackle him.

The ball carrier is ruled 'down' and play is stopped if any part of his body except his hands and feet touches the ground while he is being tackled, or if he steps off the field (goes out of bounds). If he slips and falls on his own within the field of play, however, he may continue his run.

Restarting Play

When play is stopped, the referee holds the ball at the spot where it came to rest. Play starts again parallel to this point, at the nearest set of hash marks.

Plays are started from the central area of the field to give both teams enough playing area either side of the ball.

The System of 'Downs'

To prevent one team from having the ball all the time, a system of 'downs' balances the play and makes the game more interesting.

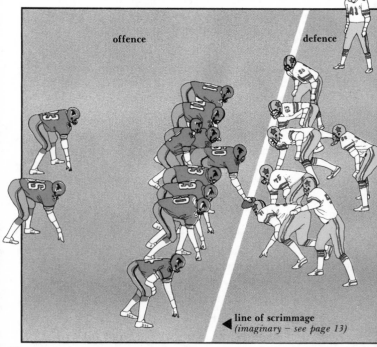

offence

defence

◀ line of scrimmage
(imaginary – see page 13)

The team with the ball (in possession) is called the OFFENCE and the team trying to get the ball is the DEFENCE.

The offence has four attempts (or downs) at advancing the ball by at least 10 yards and the players do this by either running with the ball or passing it. The defence tries to hold them back.

After each down, the game is stopped and the ball is placed on the hash marks, ready for the next down. The 10 yards can be gained on any of the four downs. When the target is reached, that team keeps the ball and starts again from first down.

Progress is made towards the opponents' end zone in this way. If they fail to achieve the 10 yards in the four downs allowed, the opposing team takes the ball and starts *their* first down.

When the state of play is said to be 'second and nine', it means that the offence is on their second attempt with 9 yards still to go. 'Third and long' – third down with more than 10 yards to go (this means they have been pushed back towards their own goal line). 'First and goal' – first down from within 10 yards of the opponents' goal line.

Generally, if the 10 yards haven't been gained after the third down, the team will elect to kick the ball. They can attempt a field goal to score points or they can 'punt' the ball into enemy territory. In punting, although the offence gives up the ball, it makes sure that the opposing team has to take possession deep in its own territory.

On the fourth down, a team may decide to try to gain the extra yardage required by passing the ball or running with it, but this will depend upon the state of play at the time.

Chain Gang

How far a team has advanced is measured along the sidelines by three officials known as the chain gang (crew). The chain is exactly 10 yards long, with a

pole at each end held by an official. One pole is placed at the point of the initial first down. The second pole is the target to be reached for the next first down.

The measurement is reset on each first down. The third official shows the number of the down being played by means of a card on a pole as shown above.

Line of Scrimmage

To start each down, the offence and defence line up facing each other across the line of scrimmage (an imaginary line running parallel to the field of play from sideline to sideline).

Scoring

A *touchdown* scores 6 points and is given when the ball is carried or passed (without bouncing) into the

end zone. The ball must break the plane of the 8 inch goal line (an imaginary wall of unlimited height). A touchdown is also scored if a player recovers a loose ball in his opponent's end zone.

plane of goal line

After a touch-down, the scoring team tries to score an extra point, or conversion, by place-kicking the ball over the crossbar and between the uprights of the posts. (In Britain, an alternative to kicking the extra point is to try to carry or pass the ball into the end zone for 2 points.)

Cleveland Browns kicking for goal against L A Raiders

When a team feels it is safer to kick for goal to gain points than to try to advance the ball by running or passing, they will try a field goal, worth 3 points. The kick can be made from anywhere on the field but is usually made from within the opponent's half. If the kick fails, the ball goes to the opposing team.

The last method of scoring is a 'safety', worth 2 points. This is awarded when an offensive player, holding the ball, is tackled in his own end zone, or when a team loses possession by the ball going out of play through their end zone. This is like an own goal in soccer.

When points are scored, the scoring team will kickoff from their own 35 yard line to give possession away. The only exception to this is following a safety, where the team conceding the safety has to kickoff from its own 20 yard line.

Duration of Play

The game is divided into four quarters of fifteen minutes. The teams change ends after the first and third quarters. Then play starts again from the field position where it finished in the previous quarter, but moving in the opposite direction. After the second quarter, the teams leave the field for a fifteen minute halftime interval.

Although actual playing time is sixty minutes, games normally last about three hours, because the official time clock is stopped whenever the ball is not in play. Each time a player is injured, each time a ball carrier goes out of bounds, and after every score or incomplete pass, the clock is stopped. It is also stopped whenever a team or official calls a time-out – each team may call up to three two and a quarter minute time-outs per half to discuss tactics.

In addition, the clock will stop when two minutes remain at the end of each half. Teams often save their time-outs until this period when changes in tactics can be more important than at any other time.

A further restriction is the forty five second clock, showing how much time the offensive team has to move the ball when the whistle blows to end the previous play.

If the scores are tied at the end of playing time, an overtime period of fifteen minutes is played to achieve a result. The first team to score in overtime wins the game. If there is no score the game remains tied. Only two time-outs per team are allowed in overtime.

PLAYERS

Since there is no limit to the number of substitutes that can be used during the game, every playing position is a specialised one.

The offensive skills of blocking, passing, catching and running with the ball are quite different from the tackling and covering duties of the defence. In the same way, each member of the special teams squad (used when kicking is needed) has his own specialist skill. Although all players must be both fast and powerful, their sizes range from the 18 stone plus linemen to kickers, who are comparatively lightly built.

OFFENCE

Before each down is played, the team goes into a 'huddle' behind the line of scrimmage to discuss their plan of action. The coaching staff on the sidelines usually send instructions to the quarterback (the general of the team) either by hand signals or by sending a substitute player onto the field. The

quarterback then calls the play to the team in coded form for simplicity and speed. (The codes used are in the team's 'playbook' which

every player is expected to know thoroughly.)

After the instructions are given, the huddle breaks up and the players are ready for play.

At the line of scrimmage, the quarterback looks at the opposing lineup and shouts out instructions to his teammates, again in code. If he sees from the opposition lineup that his team's plan of action will not work, he will shout new instructions to change the play.

The centre stands astride the ball, ready to flick it (snap it) back through his legs to the quarterback standing behind him.

The code given to the team in the huddle will tell them the lineup, the play to be used and the signal which starts the snap count (that is, the timing of the snap). At the moment the ball is snapped, the play will start.

When the whistle sounds to end the previous play, each team has only forty five seconds to go into its huddle and decide on its action before the snap takes place. Otherwise, a penalty is awarded.

Offence at Line of Scrimmage

The offence has to have at least seven players at the line of scrimmage when the ball is put into play. These players are called offensive linemen. The rest of the team behind them in the backfield are known as 'backs', and they must be at least one yard behind the line of scrimmage. Once linemen are in the down position, they are not allowed to move until the ball is moved. Only one player can be in motion behind the line (moving sideways or backwards). All other players must be stationary for at least one second before play starts.

Offensive Positions

After the snap, the interior line (made up of the centre, a guard either side of the centre and a tackle outside each guard) takes over.

These five players act as blockers either to open up holes in the defensive line for the ball carrier to run through, or to provide a wall to protect the quarterback on passing plays.

Outside the two tackles are two players called ends, each with a different function. One end usually lines up a few yards away from the tackle and is called the split end. He can catch passes as well as block. The tight end may line up outside of either tackle and does more blocking than catching. Whichever side the tight end is on is called the *strong* side.

The most important player on the team is the quarterback, because he directs the play. Once he has the ball, he must either pass it to one of his receivers, hand it to a running back (as above), or run with it himself to gain territory.

The wide receiver is usually the fastest runner and best catcher in the team, and positions himself some distance wide of the interior line.

The backs, who may be running backs, halfbacks or fullbacks, are powerful runners. They line up behind the quarterback and will block, run, pass or receive as necessary.

Depending on the play being used, the offence may use any of a number of different lineups in the backfield, such as more wide receivers, or more running backs.

Before play starts, the defensive team also goes into a huddle, at the same time as the offence, to discuss lineup and tactics for the forthcoming down.

Defensive Positions

The defence consists of linemen, linebackers and defensive backs. The linemen place themselves opposite the offensive interior line. Although there can be any number of defensive linemen, depending on the play, three or four are most common. The defensive tackles are in the centre of the line, and there are usually two. If an odd number is used however the central man is called the nose tackle, because he lines up nose to nose with the offensive centre. Outside the defensive tackles are the defensive ends.

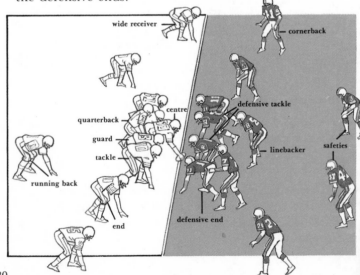

Sacking the quarterback

The defensive line has three main duties. First of all, it must force its way through the offensive line to tackle the passer.

If the passer happens to be the quarterback, this is called *sacking*.

The second duty of the defensive line is to tackle or stop any ball carrier breaking through the line of scrimmage. Lastly, the members of the line may 'bat' down or intercept passes.

Linebackers usually place themselves behind the defensive line. Their job is to chase and tackle the ball carrier if he gets through the defensive line, to be ready to defend against passes, and to be prepared to attack the quarterback (called *blitzing*).

The defensive backs operate behind the linebackers in that part of the field known as the *secondary*. Cornerbacks, who are the fastest runners in the team, cover opposing wide receivers on passing plays. The safeties are chiefly used as the last line of defence against ball carriers, and for defending against the longer passes.

Although the defence are allowed to move at the line of scrimmage, if they cross the line with any part of their bodies before the snap, a penalty is given.

SKILLS

Blocking

Blocking is the legal obstruction by offensive players of opposing players who are trying to tackle the ball carrier. It is very important for the offence to give the quarterback enough time to pass the ball, or to protect the ball carrier, giving him space to gain yardage.

When blocking, a player may use any part of his body above the knees. Holding an opponent with the hands or arms is penalised.

When blocking a running play, a player may use the upper part of his body, but not extended arms (although they may be used to protect the quarterback on a passing play).

A form of blocking that is penalised heavily is 'clipping' – that is, hitting an opponent from behind.

New York Giants (in blue) block against Pittsburgh Steelers

Passing

Passing plays usually last from five to ten seconds.

Although other backs are sometimes used, most passes in offensive plays are thrown by the quarterback.

Only one forward pass is allowed in each play, and this must be thrown from behind the line of scrimmage. If the forward pass is caught by the offence, it can be advanced until the receiver is stopped. If the forward pass is *not* caught before bouncing, it is said to be incomplete. Play then starts again at the same line of scrimmage for the next down. If the forward pass is intercepted by the defence before it bounces it may be advanced until the defender is tackled and play is stopped. His team then takes possession and brings on its offensive squad to start their own first down.

A *lateral* pass (any pass not going forward) is generally made from behind the line of scrimmage and there is no limit to the number of these allowed in each play. If a lateral pass is *not* caught by the offence, it can be intercepted before bouncing by the defence in the same way as a forward pass. If however the defence recovers it after it bounces, they can take possession from that spot.

Receiving

The pass receiver must be quick and elusive to get past defenders and interceptors, and he has to time his run exactly to meet the ball at the planned spot on the field. If the pass is to be 'complete', the receiver has to catch the ball before it bounces, must have both feet within the field of play and be in control of the ball.

The offensive interior linemen are the only players not allowed to catch passes. 'Pass interference' is also not allowed: that is, an offensive receiver and a defender must not physically try to stop each other's attempts to catch a pass.

Yardage gained by a receiver is measured from the line of scrimmage to the point he reaches while still carrying the ball.

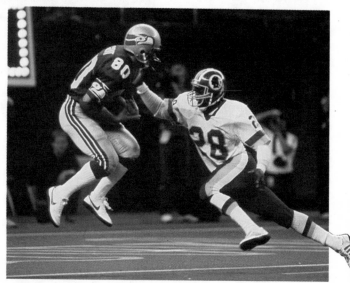

Steve Largent (Seattle Seahawks) catches a pass against Washington Redskins

Rushing
(running with the ball)

Whether he's a pass receiver or a running back, the ball carrier's aim is to hold on to the ball and gain yardage. He needs speed and agility to dodge through the gaps opened up by the blockers. He also needs power to force his way through to create his own gaps. If he loses the ball in a tackle, it is called a 'fumble' and is a free ball for anyone to collect.

Marcus Allen (LA Raiders)

Again, yardage gained by a player is the distance he achieves past the line of scrimmage.

Running plays normally take between five and seven seconds to complete.

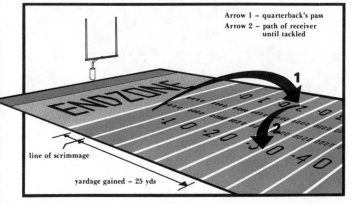

Arrow 1 – quarterback's pass
Arrow 2 – path of receiver until tackled

line of scrimmage

yardage gained – 25 yds

25

Tackling

Tackling is the main job of the defence. They must try to stop the ball carrier, or at least slow him down. Almost any type of tackle is allowed, apart from tripping with a leg, holding the opponent's facemask, kicking, kneeing or punching.

Members of the defence who are trying to reach the ball carrier are allowed to use their hands to pull or push blocking players.

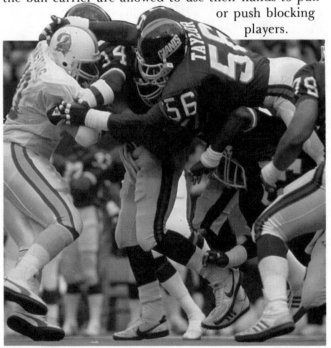

Lawrence Taylor (New York Giants) launches into a tackle

Special Teams

The *special teams* unit is used whenever kicking is needed during a game. These players are sometimes

inexperienced or substitutes, because injury is more likely in this situation, and teams won't risk their best players. For this reason, the special teams unit is also known as the 'suicide squad'!

There are two kinds of kicking: *punting* and *placekicking*.

Punting

The line of scrimmage for the punt is the same as that for running or passing plays, but there is no quarterback to receive the ball from the snap. Instead, the punter stands about 15 yards behind the line to receive the snap directly from the centre. As soon as he catches the ball, the punter drops it forward, then, before it touches the ground, kicks it as high and as far as possible. The rest of the team try to protect the punter from onrushing defenders,

but once the ball is kicked they must advance in pursuit of it. The longer the ball is in the air, the better, to give the team more time to move forward to tackle the returner. The returner cannot be tackled until he touches the ball. Alternatively, he can signal for a fair catch (see page 50). Most punts travel 40 to 50 yards in the air.

Rohn Stark (Indianapolis Colts)

Placekicking

At the kickoff (described on pages 8-9), the ball is stood upright on a plastic tee prior to kicking. In conversion and field goal attempts, however, the procedure is different.

Nine of the offensive team are placed at the line of scrimmage to protect the kicker. On a signal, the centre snaps the ball back 7 or 8 yards to a player who is down on one knee beside the spot where the kick is to be taken. On catching the ball, this player stands the ball upright, ready for the kicker's attempt at goal. Some players prefer to kick barefoot.

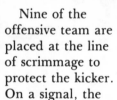

The head coaches supervise the game plan, and organise the teams from the sidelines. Here they are discussing tactics with a player

TEAM

There is a pool of 45 players on each side, from which coaches make their selection for any particular play. This pool usually consists of:

8 offensive linemen
6 receivers
5 running backs
3 quarterbacks
6 defensive linemen
8 linebackers
7 defensive backs
1 kicker
1 punter

Players' numbers

In the NFL, every player has his name and a number on his shirt. The number denotes the player's position, as shown right.

1-19 quarterbacks and kickers
20-49 running backs and defensive backs
50-59 centres and linebackers
60-79 defensive linemen and interior offensive linemen
80-89 wide receivers and tight ends
90-99 defensive linemen

OFFICIALS

Just seven officials observe and control the whole of a game in the National Football League. They are the referee, umpire, head linesman, line judge, field judge, back judge and side judge. They all wear black and white striped shirts, but the referee can be identified by his black cap.

Each official carries a small weighted piece of yellow material, called a flag. When a foul is spotted, the flag is thrown to the ground in that direction. The term 'a flag on the play' means that a foul has been committed. Play generally continues until the ball is dead. Then the officials decide on the penalty for the foul. The referee informs the players and spectators of the penalty awarded by means of one of the arm signals shown here, and points towards the offending team's goal line.

Pass Juggled Inbounds, Caught Out of Bounds

Illegal Forward Pass

Interference With Forward Pass or Fair Catch

Invalid Fair Catch Signal

Loss of Down

Illegal Motion at Snap

Crawling, Pushing, or Helping Runner

Unsportsmanlike Conduct

Tripping

Illegal Block Crackback

Delay of Game

No Time Out or
Time In With Whistle

Offside or Encroaching

Holding

Penalty Refused,
Incomplete Pass, Play
Over, or Missed Field Goal

Touchdown, Field Goal,
or Successful Try

Ball Illegally Touched,
Kicked, or Batted

Illegal Use of Hands,
Arms, or Body

Illegal Contact

Intentional
Grounding of Pass

Illegal Cut or Blocking
Below the Waist

Touching a Forward Pass
or Scrimmage Kick

Player Disqualified

Ineligible Receiver or
Ineligible Member of
Kicking Team Downfield

False Start, Illegal Shift,
Procedure, or Formation

Safety

Time Out

Dead Ball or Neutral
Zone Established

First Down

Personal Foul

Penalties

In most other ball games, a foul usually means a loss of possession, but in American football it is penalised by a loss of yardage against the offending team. This means that the ball is moved by the distance of the penalty towards their goal line. A loss of down may be awarded if the offenders are the team in possession, and sometimes a penalty can involve both yardage and down.

Although the referee's rulebook contains over sixty penalties which may occur during a game, there are basically four types:

pulling opponent by the facemask

defensive pass interference

(a) 5 yard penalty – for minor offences

(b) 10 yards – for physical contact or technical violations

(c) 15 yards – more serious offences which could mean that other players might be hurt

(d) Serious violent conduct may result in a player being sent off, but his team can replace him to maintain a full squad on the field

The National Football League

In 1922, eleven clubs formed the NFL. A rival league, the All American Football Conference (AAFC), was formed in 1946 and merged with the NFL in 1950. In 1960, another league came into existence, the American Football League (AFL). In that same year, Pete Rozelle became the NFL commissioner. Rozelle managed to get television contracts for games, thus putting the league on a sound financial basis.

Pete Rozelle

On 8th June 1966, following fierce competition to sign college players, the two leagues merged. From that day on, there was to be a common college draft (see page 34), and an annual championship game between the leagues (now called conferences), known as the Super Bowl.

From 1970, when the full merger took effect, the NFL consisted of two leagues, the National Football Conference (NFC) and the American Football Conference (AFC). Each league has fourteen teams spread over three divisions – Eastern, Central and Western.

The Draft

The draft system was started over fifty years ago, in 1936, so that teams could choose new players from the best graduating college players each year. The team with the worst record in the league from the previous season get the first pick of these players. The team with the best record, the Super Bowl champions, get the last choice. This means that the playing strength of the teams in the league is balanced so that the weakest becomes stronger. In

addition to getting the last choice, the Super Bowl champions are also given a tougher league schedule for the next season.

Draft day is usually in late April and by the time it takes place, each team has usually found out all about the players available. Clubs already know which areas of their squad need strengthening and choose accordingly. Often they will trade draft picks for experienced players from other teams.

There are twelve rounds of draft picks in which each team makes a selection (12 rounds × 28 teams = 336 players eligible). Some teams may have more than one pick in a round, or none at all, depending on what trading has been done. Team representatives at the draft are in constant touch with their own clubs.

Once chosen, the draft picks then go to their team's summer training camp to prepare for the new season. Players not selected in the draft are called 'free agents', and may offer their services to any club.

Training Camp

To prepare for the new season, all players report to their club's summer camp, which usually lasts all through July.

In the first two weeks, the draft choices (called *rookies*) are given many tests before the established players (*veterans*) arrive for the last two weeks.

Each training complex is nearly always equipped with a training field, gymnasium, weight room, swimming pool and medical rooms. Players are closely supervised, and usually sleep in dormitories on the site. They are tested for speed, endurance and power, and have

several medical checkups while this is going on. Specialist coaches put the various groups of players – receivers, linemen, etc – through their own training schedules. In a full day at camp, the players spend part of the time in training, and the rest in the classroom where tactics are developed. All players must learn the playbook, which contains all the coach's tactics and plays – as many as 150 or more.

At the start of the camp more than a hundred players may attend, but this is cut down to a forty five man roster for the beginning of the season. In August the team plays four or five preseason games, and the league games start in early September.

AMERICAN FOOTBALL CONFERENCE

EASTERN DIVISION

Buffalo Bills

BILLS ™

Founded: 1959
Stadium: Rich Stadium
Capacity: 80,290
Surface: Astroturf
Colours: Scarlet, white
and royal blue

Indianapolis Colts

COLTS ™

Founded: 1952
Previous
name: Baltimore Colts
Stadium: Hoosier Dome
Capacity: 60,127
Surface: Astroturf
Colours: Royal blue, white
and silver

Miami Dolphins

Dolphins ™

Founded: 1965
Stadium: Joe Robbie Stadium
Capacity: 75,500
Surface: Grass
Colours: Aqua, coral and white

New England Patriots

Founded: 1959
Previous name: Boston Patriots
Stadium: Sullivan Stadium
Capacity: 61,000
Surface: Superturf
Colours: Red, white and blue

New York Jets

Founded: 1959
Previous name: New York Titans
Stadium: Giants Stadium, New Jersey (shared with New York Giants)
Capacity: 76,891
Surface: Astroturf
Colours: Kelly green and white

CENTRAL DIVISION

Cincinnati Bengals

Founded: 1967
Stadium: Riverfront Stadium
Capacity: 59,754
Surface: Astroturf
Colours: Black, orange and white

Cleveland Browns

BROWNS™

Founded: 1946
Stadium: Cleveland Stadium
Capacity: 80,098
Surface: Grass
Colours: Seal brown, orange and white

Houston Oilers

OILERS™

Founded: 1959
Stadium: Astrodome
Capacity: 50,496
Surface: Astroturf
Colours: Scarlet, Columbia blue and white

Pittsburgh Steelers

Steelers™

Founded: 1933
Previous name: Pittsburgh Pirates
Stadium: Three Rivers Stadium
Capacity: 59,000
Surface: Astroturf
Colours: Black and gold

WESTERN DIVISION

Denver Broncos

BRONCOS™

Founded: 1959
Stadium: Mile High Stadium
Capacity: 75,100
Surface: Grass
Colours: Orange, blue and white

Kansas City Chiefs

CHIEFS ™

Founded: 1959
Previous name: Dallas Texans
Stadium: Arrowhead Stadium
Capacity: 78,067
Surface: Astroturf
Colours: Red, gold and white

Los Angeles Raiders

RAIDERS ™

Founded: 1960
Previous name: Oakland Raiders
Stadium: Los Angeles Memorial Coliseum
Capacity: 92,516
Surface: Grass
Colours: Silver and black

San Diego Chargers

CHARGERS ™

Founded: 1959
Previous name: Los Angeles Chargers
Stadium: San Diego Jack Murphy Stadium
Capacity: 60,100
Surface: Grass
Colours: Blue, gold and white

Seattle Seahawks

Seahawks ™

Founded: 1972
Previous name: Seattle Professional Football Inc
Stadium: Kingdome
Capacity: 64,984
Surface: Astroturf
Colours: Blue, green and silver

NATIONAL FOOTBALL CONFERENCE

EASTERN DIVISION

Dallas Cowboys

COWBOYS™

Founded: 1960
Stadium: Texas Stadium
Capacity: 63,749
Surface: Texas turf
Colours: Royal blue, metallic silver blue and white

New York Giants

GIANTS™

Founded: 1925
Stadium: Giants Stadium, New Jersey (with New York Jets)
Capacity: 76,891
Surface: Astroturf
Colours: Blue, red and white

Philadelphia Eagles

EAGLES™

Founded: 1933
Previous name: Frankford Yellowjackets
Stadium: Veterans Stadium
Capacity: 69,417
Surface: Astroturf
Colours: Kelly green, white and silver

Phoenix Cardinals

CARDINALS ™

Founded: 1899
Previous names: Racine Cardinals, Chicago Cardinals, Cards-Pitts, St Louis Cardinals
Stadium: Sun Devil Stadium
Capacity: 70,021
Surface: Grass
Colours: Cardinal red, black and white

Washington Redskins

REDSKINS ™

Founded: 1932
Previous names: Boston Braves, Boston Redskins
Stadium: Robert F. Kennedy Stadium
Capacity: 55,750
Surface: Grass
Colours: Burgundy and gold

CENTRAL DIVISION

Chicago Bears

BEARS ™

Founded: 1920
Previous names: Decatur Staleys, Chicago Staleys
Stadium: Soldier Field
Capacity: 65,790
Surface: Grass
Colours: Orange, navy blue and white

Detroit Lions

LIONS™

Founded: 1930
Previous
name: Portsmouth Spartans
Stadium: Pontiac Silverdome
Capacity: 80,638
Surface: Astroturf
Colours: Honolulu blue
and silver

Green Bay Packers

PACKERS™

Founded: 1919
Stadium: (a) Lambeau Field
(Green Bay) and
(b) Milwaukee County
Stadium
Capacity: (a) 57,063; (b) 55,976
Surface: Grass (both)
Colours: Dark green, gold
and white

Minnesota Vikings

VIKINGS™

Founded: 1960
Stadium: Hubert H. Humphrey
Metrodome
Capacity: 62,345
Surface: Superturf
Colours: Purple, white and gold

Tampa Bay Buccaneers

BUCCANEERS™

Founded: 1975
Stadium: Tampa Stadium
Capacity: 74,315
Surface: Grass
Colours: Florida orange, white
and red

WESTERN DIVISION

Atlanta Falcons

FALCONS ™

Founded: 1965
Stadium: Atlanta-Fulton
County Stadium
Capacity: 60,748
Surface: Grass
Colours: Red, black, silver
and white

Los Angeles Rams

RAMS ™

Founded: 1937
*Previous
name:* Cleveland Rams
Stadium: Anaheim Stadium
Capacity: 69,007
Surface: Grass
Colours: Royal blue, gold
and white

New Orleans Saints

SAINTS ™

Founded: 1966
Stadium: Louisiana Superdome
Capacity: 69,723
Surface: Astroturf
Colours: Old gold, black
and white

San Francisco 49ers

49ERS ™

Founded: 1946
Stadium: Candlestick Park
Capacity: 61,499
Surface: Grass
Colours: 49er gold and scarlet

SUPER BOWL

In the NFL, there are two conferences, each with three divisions. Within the divisions, every team plays sixteen games (eight at home and eight away) between September and Christmas. It plays the other teams in its division twice, then the rest of its games are against other teams in the NFL.

At the end of the league season, the team with the most wins becomes the division champion. If more than one team has the same number of wins, a tie break system is used to decide the winner.

The champion of each division goes through to the playoff semifinals. There are therefore three division winners in each conference. One further team in each conference goes through to the playoff semifinals. This is the winner of a 'wild card' game between the two teams in the conference with the next best records to the winners of the divisions.

The playoffs last from Christmas to mid January. The AFC champions then play the NFC champions in the Super Bowl at the end of January.

From the opening day of the season, winning the Super Bowl is every team's target.

Super Bowl Trophy

Conference Playoffs

Super Bowl

The Vince Lombardi
(Super Bowl) Trophy is
made of silver. It is
20 inches high and weighs
7 lbs. It was named after
the coach of the Green
Bay Packers, the team
that won the first two
Super Bowls.

Super Bowl Results				
I	Green Bay	35	Kansas City	10
II	Green Bay	33	Oakland	14
III	New York Jets	16	Baltimore	7
IV	Kansas City	23	Minnesota	7
V	Baltimore	16	Dallas	13
VI	Dallas	24	Miami	3
VII	Miami	14	Washington	7
VIII	Miami	24	Minnesota	7
IX	Pittsburgh	16	Minnesota	6
X	Pittsburgh	21	Dallas	17
XI	Oakland	32	Minnesota	14
XII	Dallas	27	Denver	10
XIII	Pittsburgh	35	Dallas	31
XIV	Pittsburgh	31	L A Rams	19
XV	Oakland	27	Philadelphia	10
XVI	San Francisco	26	Cincinnati	21
XVII	Washington	27	Miami	17
XVIII	L A Raiders	38	Washington	9
XIX	San Francisco	38	Miami	16
XX	Chicago	46	New England	10
XXI	New York Giants	39	Denver	20
XXII	Washington	42	Denver	10

Each member of the Super Bowl winning team receives a very special reward, a commemorative ring. Players value these rings even more than the team trophy, as a lifelong reminder of their achievement.

Commemorative ring for San Francisco 49ers for Super Bowl XIX

AFC/NFC Pro Bowl

One of the highest honours a player can receive is to be asked to play in the AFC/NFC Pro Bowl, which usually takes place in Hawaii, a week after the Super Bowl. This game is between a selected team from the AFC and one from the NFC, and all the players have been nominated by their fellow professionals within the conference.

Pro Football Hall of Fame

The greatest honour of all is to be elected to the Pro Football Hall of Fame in Canton, Ohio, where the original meeting to set up the NFL was held in 1920. The Hall of Fame started life as one building in September 1963, but there are now four buildings in the complex and it is a major tourist attraction. To be eligible for election, a player must have been retired for five years at least. Coaches can be selected on retirement, and administrators can be still in office. Only five or six people are elected each year. By August 1988, there were 144 members.

★ ★ ★ ★ ★ ★ ★ ★ ★ ★ INDEX ★ ★ ★ ★ ★ ★ ★ ★ ★ ★

	page
AFC/NFC Pro Bowl	48
All American Football Conference (AAFC)	33
Allen, Marcus	25
American Football Conference (AFC)	33, 37, 38, 46, 48
American Football League (AFL)	33
American Professional Football Association	front endpaper
Association Football (soccer)	front endpaper, 14
Atlanta Falcons	8, 37, 45
ball	4/5
Baltimore Colts	47
blitzing	21
blocking	9, 16, 19, 22, 25, 26, 51
breaking the plane	13
Buffalo Bills	37, 38
Camp, Walter	front endpaper
chain & pole	12
chain gang (crew)	12
Chicago Bears	37, 43, 47
Cincinnati Bengals	37, 39, 47
Cleveland Browns	14, 37, 40
clipping	22
coaches	16, 28, 29, 36, 48
code	16, 17
Dallas Cowboys	37, 42, 47
defence	8, 11, 13, 16, 20, 21, 23, 24, 26, 27, 50
defensive positions	
– backs	20, 21, 29, 50
– cornerbacks	21
– ends	20
– linebackers	20, 21, 29
– linemen	20, 29
– nose tackle	20
– safeties	21
– tackles	20
Denver Broncos	37, 40, 47
Detroit Lions	37, 44, 49
downs	10, 11, 12, 13, 16, 20, 23, 32
draft	33, 34, 35
duration of play	15
Ellis, William Webb	front endpaper

	page
equipment	6-7
field of play	front endpaper 4/5, 8, 9, 10, 11, 13, 14 15, 16, 21, 24, 28, 30, 32
flag	30
free agents	35
free ball	25, 50
goal posts	4/5, 13
Green Bay Packers	37, 44, 47
Hall of Fame	48
Harvard University	front endpaper
helmet	7
history of the game	front endpaper
Houston Oilers	37, 40
huddle	16, 17, 20
Indianapolis Colts	27, 37, 38
Kansas City Chiefs	37, 41, 47
kicker	8, 16, 28, 29
kicking	front endpaper, 8, 11 13, 14, 16, 26, 27, 28
kickoff	9, 14, 28, 51
L. A. Raiders	14, 25, 37, 41, 47
L. A. Rams	37, 45, 47
Largent, Steve	24
lateral pass	23
line of scrimmage	13, 16, 17, 18 21, 23, 24, 25, 27, 28, 50, 51
Lombardi, Vince	47
loose ball	13
Luckhurst, Mick	8
McGill University	front endpaper
Miami Dolphins	37, 38, 47
Minnesota Vikings	37, 44, 47
Montana, Joe	23
National Football Conference (NFC)	33, 37, 42, 46, 48
National Football League (NFL)	front endpaper, 29, 30 33, 37, 46, 48
New England Patriots	37, 39, 47
New Orleans Saints	37, 45
New York Giants	22, 26, 37, 42, 47
New York Jets	37, 39, 47

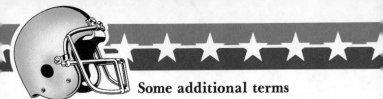

Some additional terms

audible quarterback calls a change of play at the line of scrimmage

bomb a long pass downfield by the quarterback

coverage methods used by the defence to mark offensive players

delay of game expiry of 45 seconds between the whistle to end the play and the snap

dime defence six defensive backs in a pass defence formation; a nickel defence uses five

encroachment jumping forward from the line of scrimmage and touching an opponent before the snap

fair catch signalling by holding up one arm by a punt returner to prevent being tackled. Ball may not be advanced beyond the catch

fake quarterback pretending to do something to fool the defence

fly pattern the route taken by a wide receiver

gadget play a trick play

handoff putting the ball in the running back's hands

I-formation two running backs line up directly behind the quarterback on a play

man-to-man defensive system where each player marks a possible receiver on a passing play

muff touching a free ball following a fumble, but then losing possession of it

neutral zone space between the ball and the two teams at the line of scrimmage

offside a lineman of either team who crosses the line of scrimmage before the snap

onside kick a short kickoff, which must travel at least 10 yards, where a team is seeking to regain possession

pass rush defensive linemen trying to prevent the quarterback from making a pass

personal foul serious violent conduct

play action a fake handoff to a running back by a quarterback before passing

pocket a protective area created by blockers for the quarterback

quarterback sneak used when short yardage is required in which the quarterback keeps possession and rushes through the line of scrimmage

roughing the kicker (or quarterback) illegal contact after a play has been made

shift movement of offensive players to new formation before the snap

shotgun quarterback stands a few yards back to receive the snap. Usually used on a passing play

sweep a running back moves to the outside of the line of scrimmage before moving upfield

T-formation three running backs set behind the quarterback in the shape of a 'T'

two minute offence using plays to advance up the field quickly if points are needed, and rushing plays to use up time if the team is winning, usually in the last two minutes of each half

Pontiac Silverdome, indoor home of the Detroit Lions